Famous & Fun Classics
11 Appealing Piano Arrangements
Carol Matz

Famous & Fun Classics, Book 5, is a wonderful introduction to the timeless masterworks of the great composers. The collection includes arrangements of themes from symphonic, operatic and keyboard literature, carefully selected for their appeal to students. These intermediate arrangements can be used as a supplement to any method. Book 5 introduces sixteenth notes, and features arrangements in key signatures with up to two sharps or one flat. At the end of the book, you will find pages "About the Composers," which contain interesting biographical information in language that is easy to understand. Enjoy your experience with these musical masterpieces.

Carol Matz

La donna e mobile

(from the opera *Rigoletto*)

Giuseppe Verdi (1813–1901)
Arr. by Carol Matz

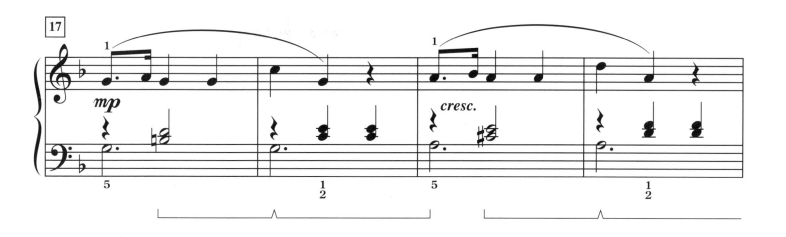

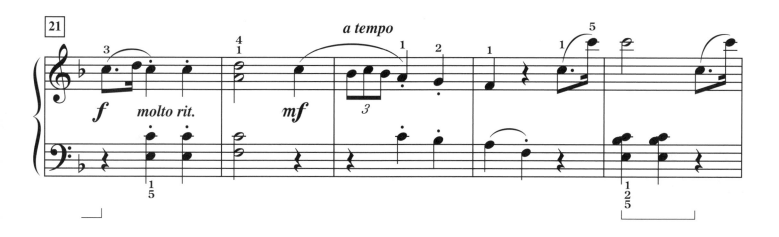

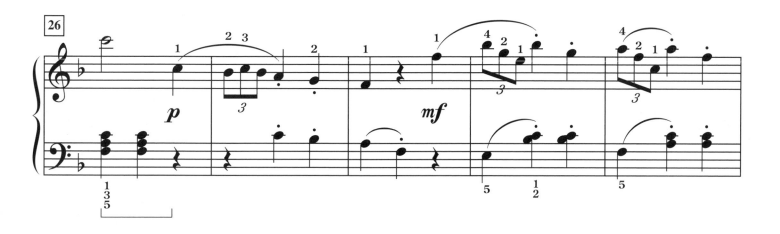

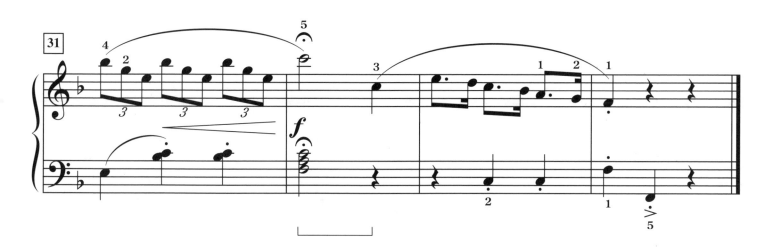

The Swan

(from *The Carnival of the Animals*)

Camille Saint-Saëns (1835–1921)
Arr. by Carol Matz

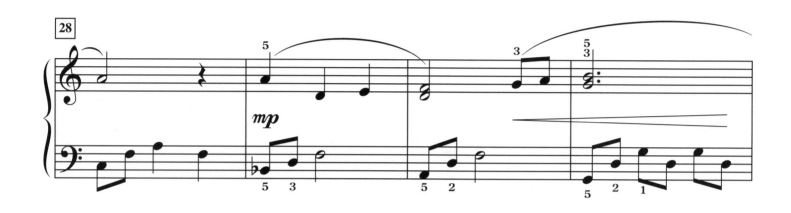

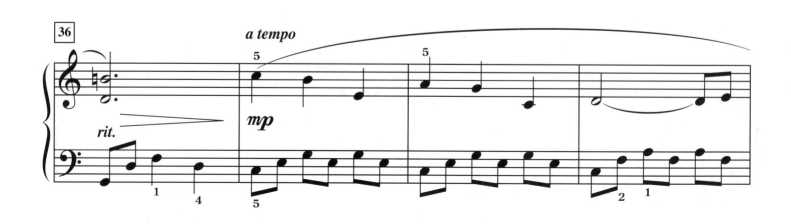

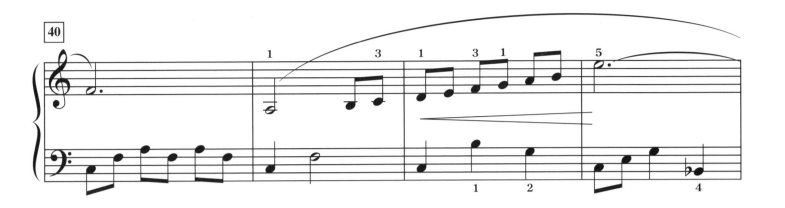

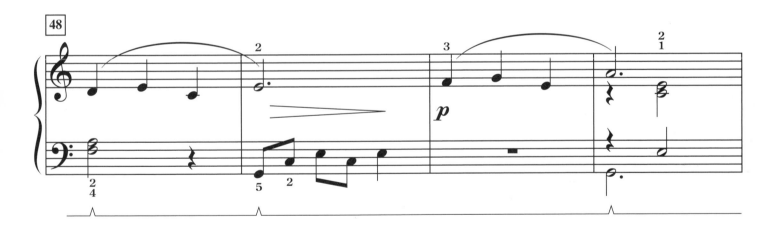

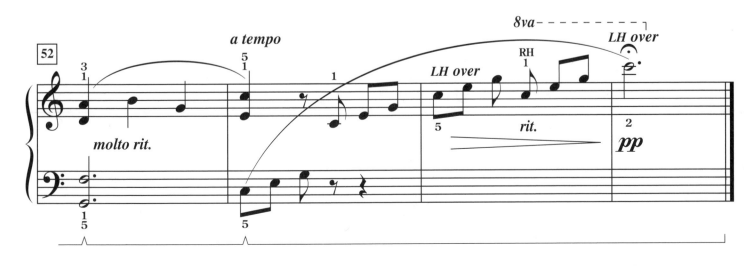

Funeral March of a Marionette

Charles Gounod (1818–1893)
Arr. by Carol Matz

Moderately

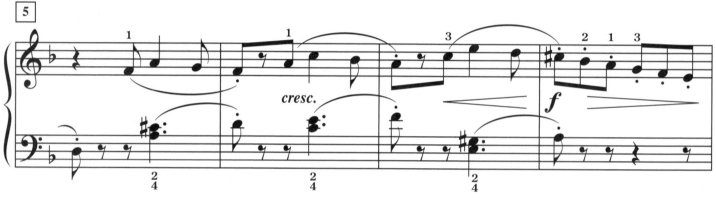

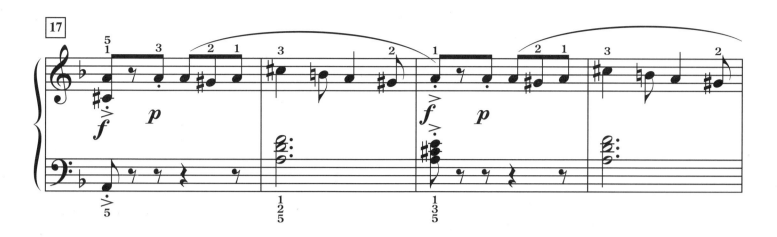

Theme from
Piano Concerto No. 1

Peter Ilyich Tchaikovsky (1840–1893)
Arr. by Carol Matz

Habañera

(from the opera *Carmen*)

Georges Bizet (1838–1875)
Arr. by Carol Matz

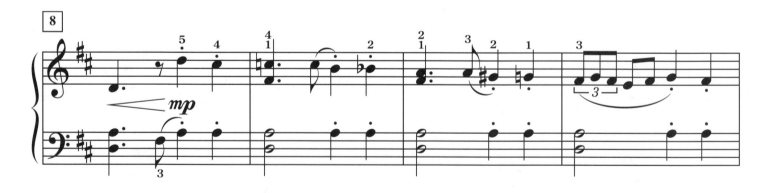

Un bel dì
(One Fine Day)
(from the opera *Madame Butterfly*)

Giacomo Puccini (1858–1924)
Arr. by Carol Matz

In the Hall of the Mountain King

(from *Peer Gynt Suite*)

Edvard Grieg (1843–1907)
Arr. by Carol Matz

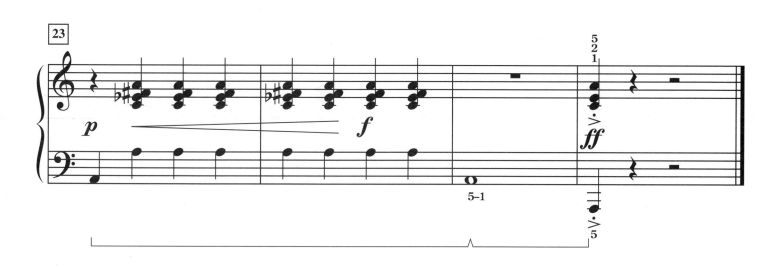

Clair de lune

(from *Suite Bergamasque*)

Claude Debussy (1862–1918)
Arr. by Carol Matz

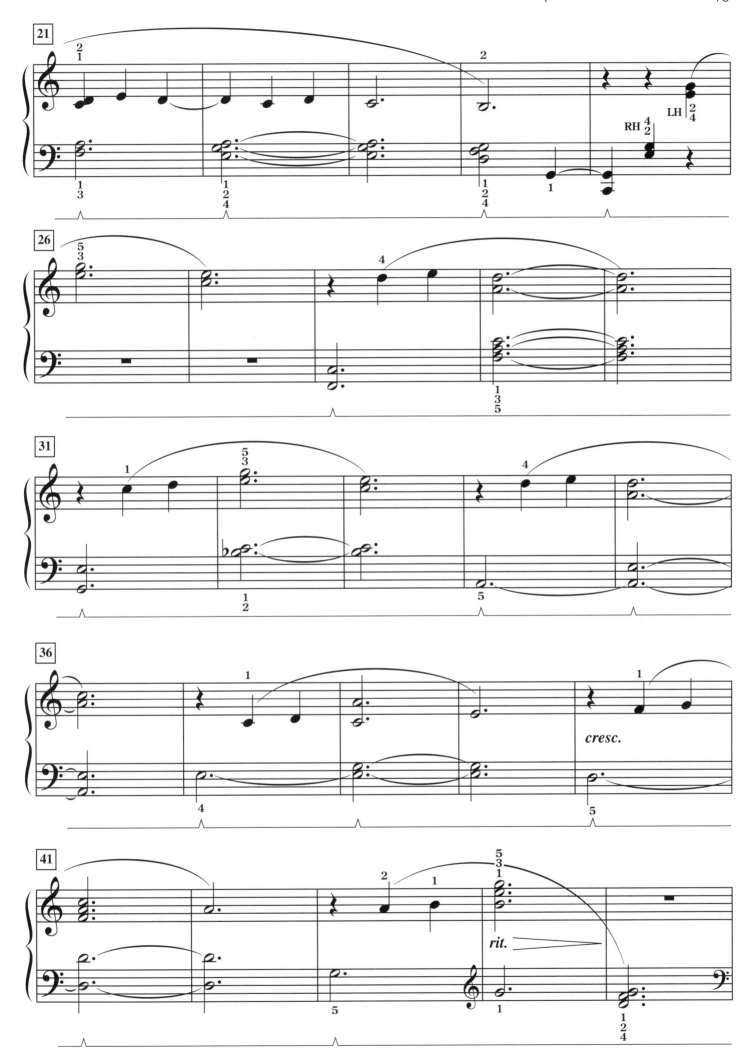

Ave Maria

(based on Bach's *Prelude No. 1, BWV 846*)

Charles Gounod (1818–1893)
(Johann Sebastian Bach; 1685–1750)
Arr. by Carol Matz

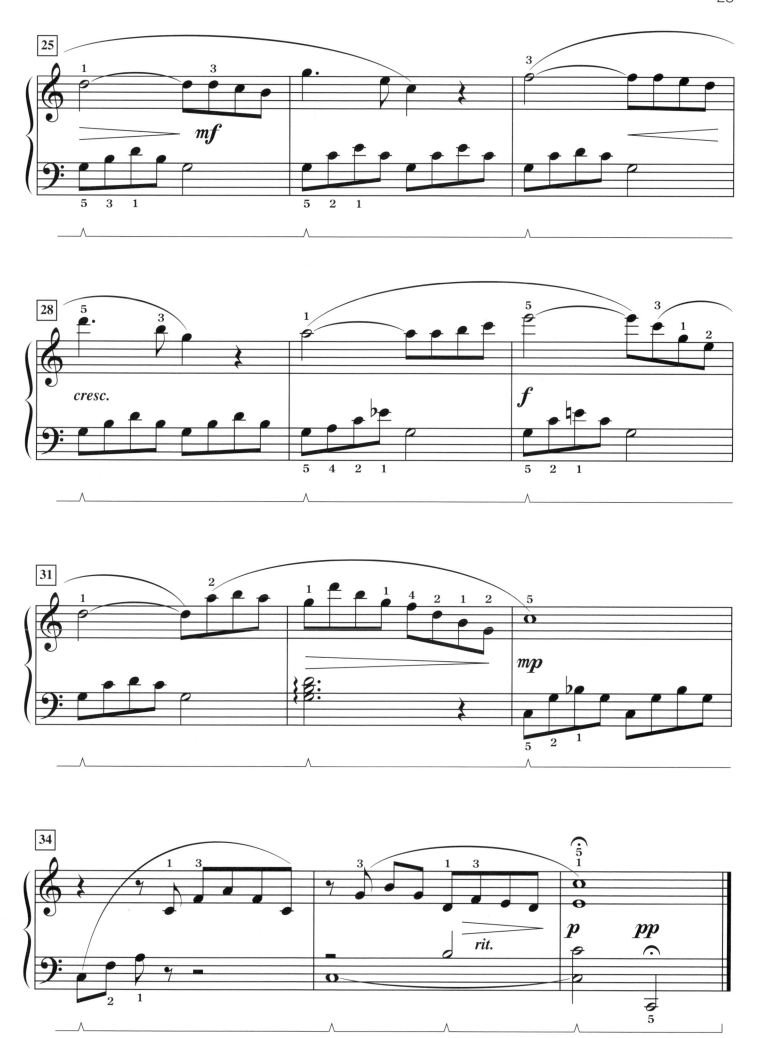

Hornpipe

(from *Water Music Suite*)

George Frideric Handel (1685–1759)
Arr. by Carol Matz

Canon

Johann Pachelbel (1653–1706)
Arr. by Carol Matz

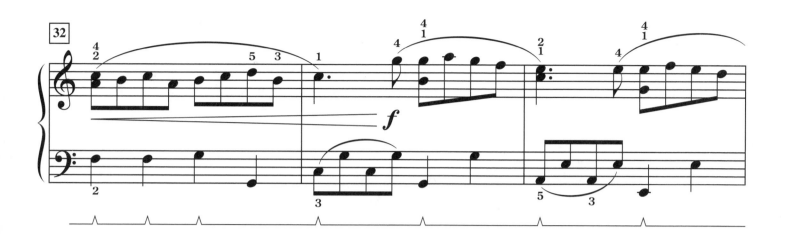

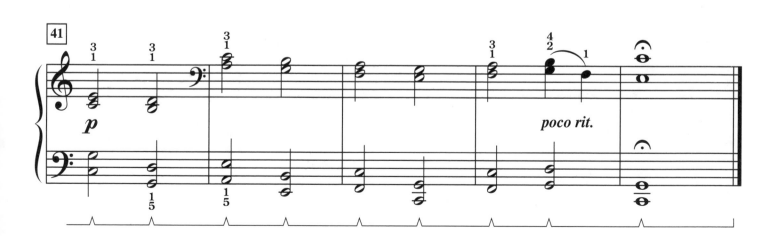

About the Composers

Johann Sebastian Bach
Born March 21, 1685; died July 28, 1750
Nationality: German

Bach was a great organist and church musician who composed all kinds of pieces for church services, keyboard instruments, orchestras and more. Besides his music, Bach is famous for having had 20 children! Four of his children grew up to become famous composers.

Georges Bizet
Born October 25, 1838; died June 3, 1875
Nationality: French

Both of Bizet's parents were musicians. His father gave Georges his first music lessons at the age of four. Bizet became an accomplished pianist, and went on to study composition. In his lifetime, he wrote over 150 piano pieces, a symphony, operas and other works. His masterpiece, the opera *Carmen,* is performed throughout the world.

Claude Debussy
Born August 22, 1862; died March 25, 1918
Nationality: French

When Debussy was a boy, his father owned a china shop and his mother was a seamstress. Since they did not have much money, Debussy's godparents paid for his piano lessons. He eventually attended the Paris Conservatory, but failed his piano tests and decided to compose, for which he won many prizes. Debussy became famous for many of his orchestral works and piano pieces.

Charles Gounod
Born June 17, 1818; died October 18, 1893
Nationality: French

Gounod's mother was his first piano teacher. He began composing at the age of 12, and studied at the Paris Conservatory. He also lived in both Italy and England where he studied music, conducted and composed operas. Gounod's *Funeral March of a Marionette* was used as the theme music for the television show *Alfred Hitchcock Presents*, which featured horror and suspense stories.

Edvard Grieg

Born June 15, 1843; died September 4, 1907
Nationality: Norwegian

Grieg grew up in Norway, and then moved to Germany to study music when he was a teenager. He became a wonderful pianist and gave concerts all over Europe, but every summer he went back to Norway to compose. Many of his pieces are based on the sounds of Norwegian folk music.

George Frideric Handel

Born February 23, 1685; died April 14, 1759
Nationality: German-born, lived in England

Because his father insisted that he become a lawyer, Handel practiced the keyboard in secret. Finally, his father heard him play the organ for a duke, who made sure that Handel got the finest musical training. Handel eventually moved to England where he became a huge success writing operas and oratorios.

Johann Pachelbel

Born September 1, 1653; died March 9, 1706
Nationality: German

Pachelbel was a German composer and organist who is best known for his *Canon in D*, which is often played at weddings. Johann Sebastian Bach's older brother was Pachelbel's organ student. In fact, Pachelbel was close friends with many members of the Bach family. In addition to the *Canon in D*, Pachelbel wrote many pieces for the Lutheran church, as well as numerous violin sonatas.

Giacomo Puccini

Born December 22, 1858; died November 29, 1924
Nationality: Italian

For generations, Puccini's family worked as church composers and organists. At first, he followed their example by working in the church, but one night he walked 13 miles to see Verdi's opera *Aida,* and he realized his true passion was opera. He went on to become one of the greatest opera composers of all time.

Camille Saint-Saëns

Born October 9, 1835; died December 16, 1921
Nationality: French

At the age of three, Saint-Saëns could already read and write, and began composing music. He eventually performed all over the world, traveling with his servant and his pet dogs. In his lifetime, Saint-Saëns composed more than 300 works and served as a church organist for over 20 years.

(continued)

About the Composers (continued)

Peter Ilyich Tchaikovsky
Born May 7, 1840; died November 6, 1893
Nationality: Russian

Although Tchaikovsky began studying music as a young boy, he ended up going to law school and getting a job with the government. However, Tchaikovsky never lost his love of music and he eventually taught and composed music for a living. In 1891, he traveled to New York to conduct his music at the opening of the famous Carnegie Hall.

Giuseppe Verdi
Born October 10, 1813; died January 27, 1901
Nationality: Italian

Verdi was one of the greatest composers of opera. He became famous for his sense of drama and his powerful melodies. Verdi was a very patriotic Italian; both he and his music became symbols of Italy's struggle for independence from Austrian rule. When Verdi died, he was very rich and famous.